AF091782

# This Notebook Belongs To

________________________________________

www.ingramcontent.com/pod-product-compliance
Lightning Source LLC
LaVergne TN
LVHW060209080526
838202LV00052B/4216
* 9 7 8 2 2 3 1 8 5 0 5 8 6 *